ADULT COLORING BOOK
by Two Hoots Coloring

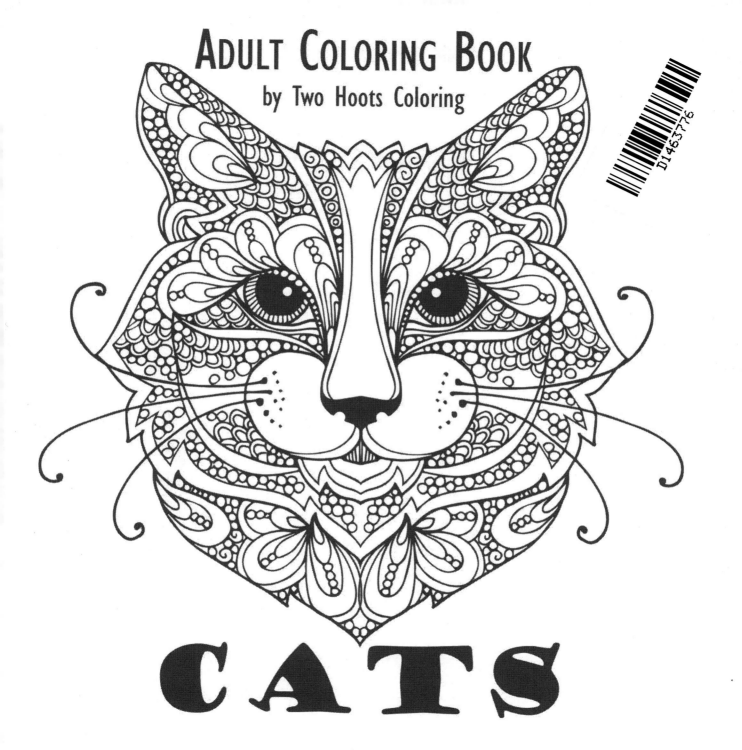

CATS

Tips For Using This Book

1. We have printed the pictures on one side of the page only for the protection of each individual picture. A sheet of loose paper under the page you are working on will offer additional protection to the pages underneath.

2. Start with any page that grabs your interest - who says you need to start at the beginning?

3. Be free and color how YOU desire. There is no "wrong" way.

4. For a stress-relieving coloring experience, reduce noise and other distractions while coloring. Coloring with focus and intention is calming and nourishing for your spirit.

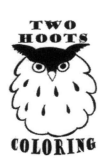

Adult Coloring Book: Cats
By: Two Hoots Coloring
Copyright © 2015

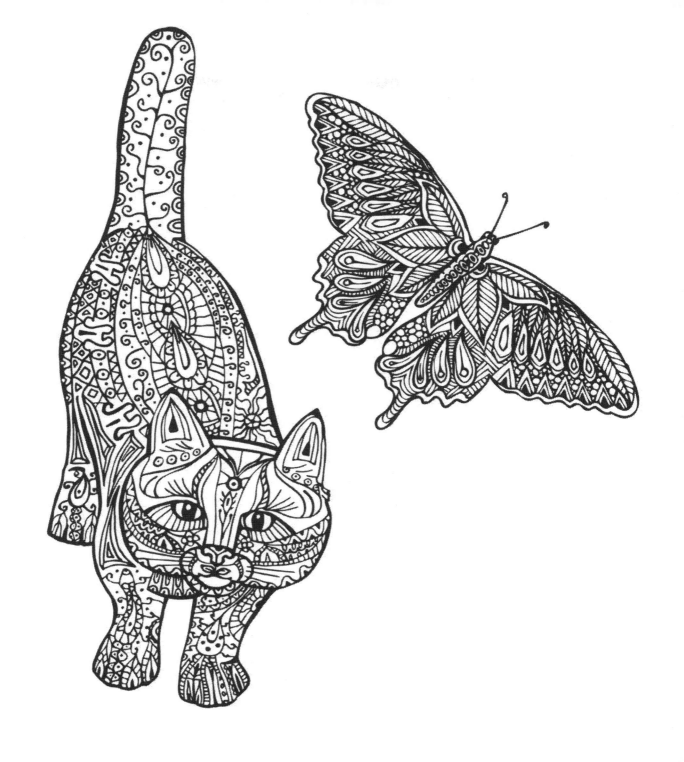

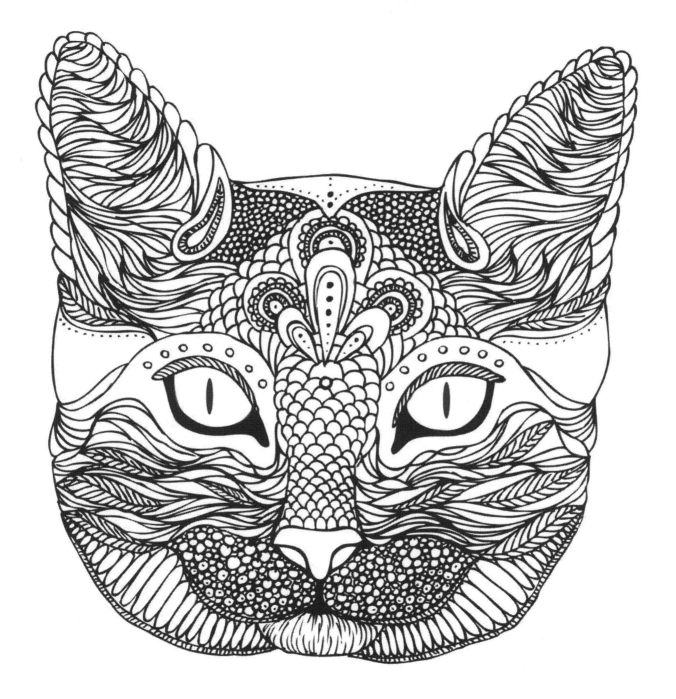

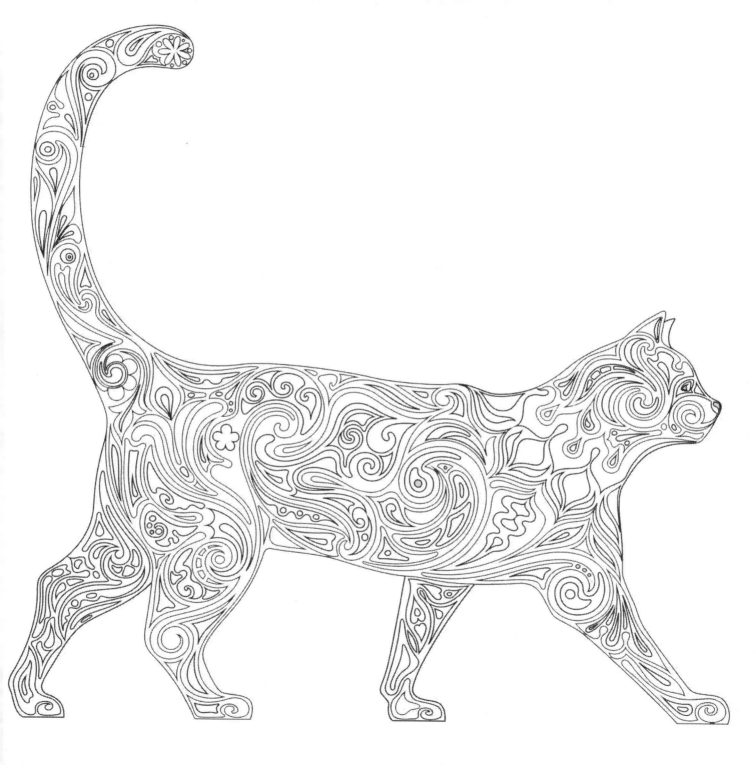

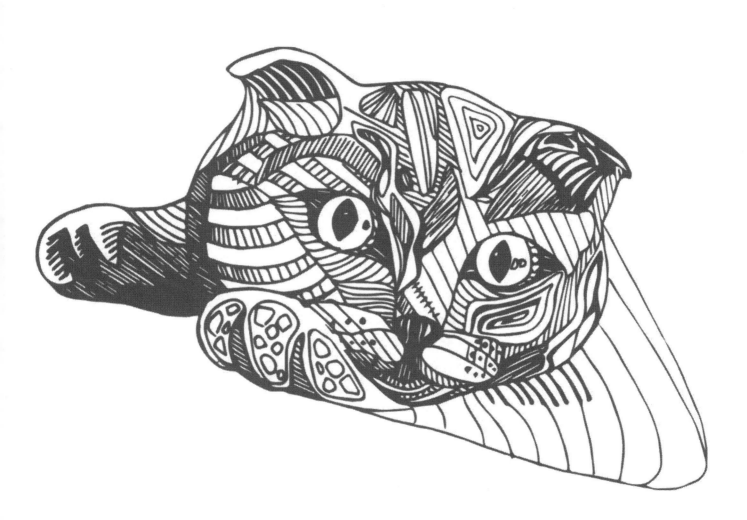

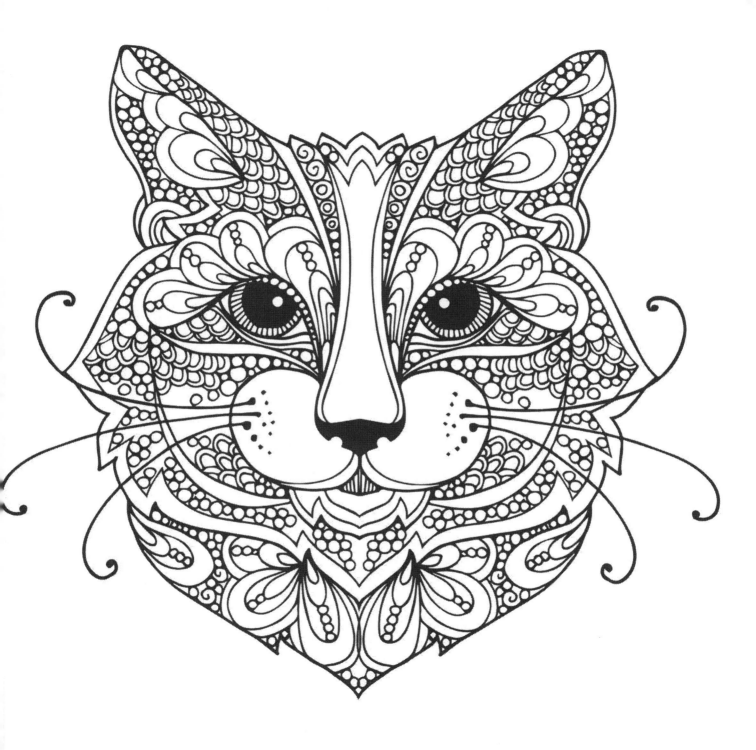

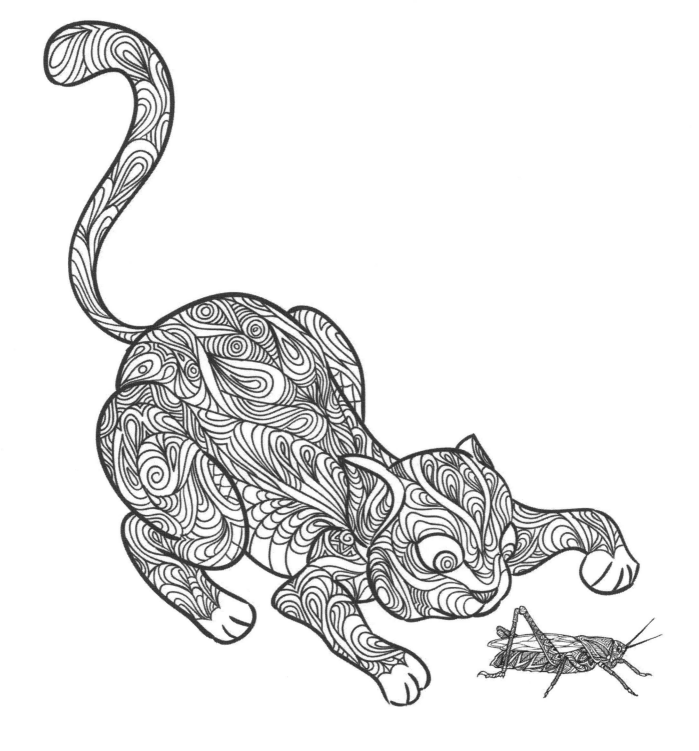

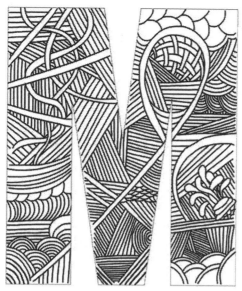
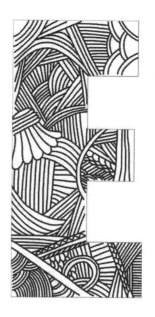
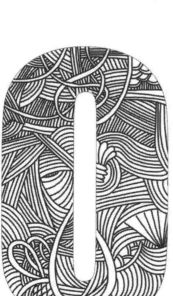
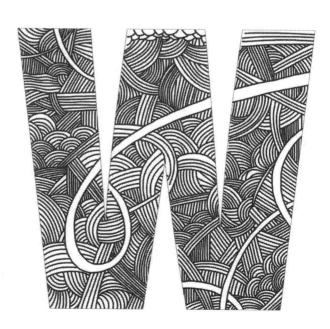

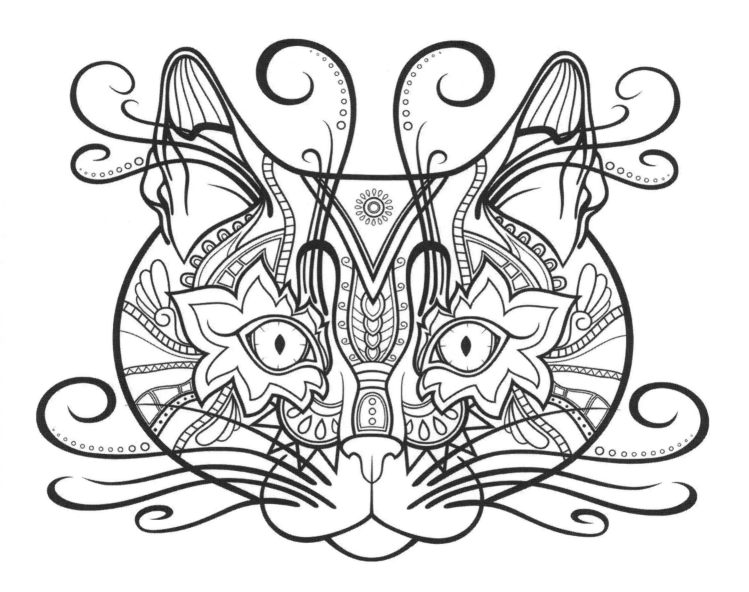

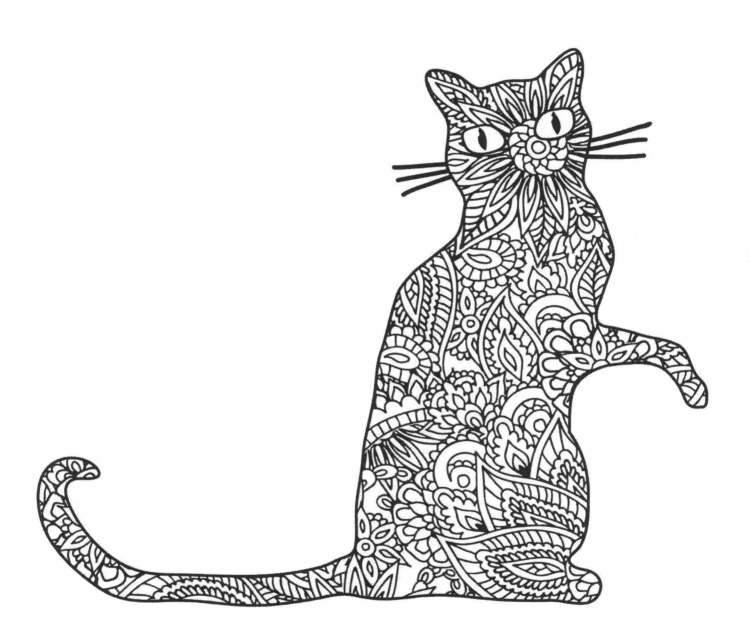

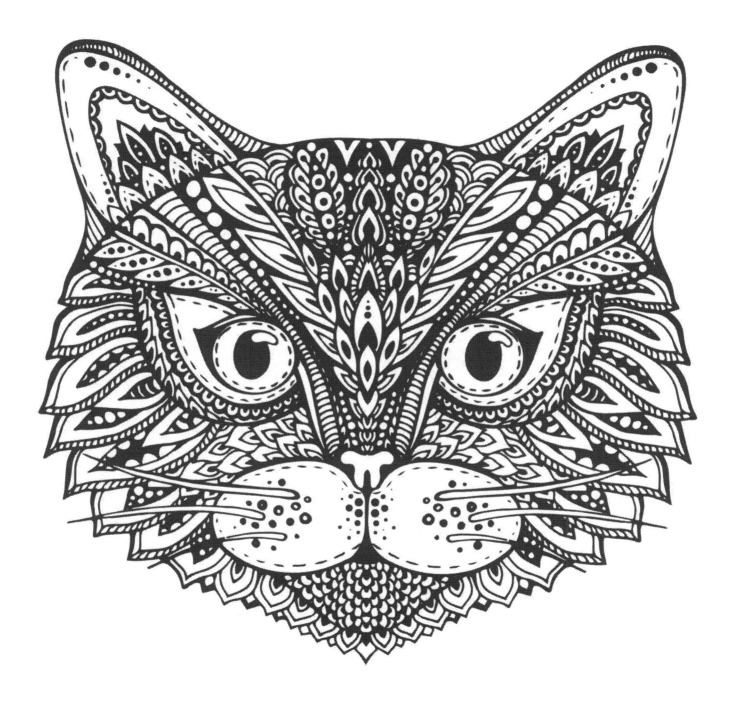

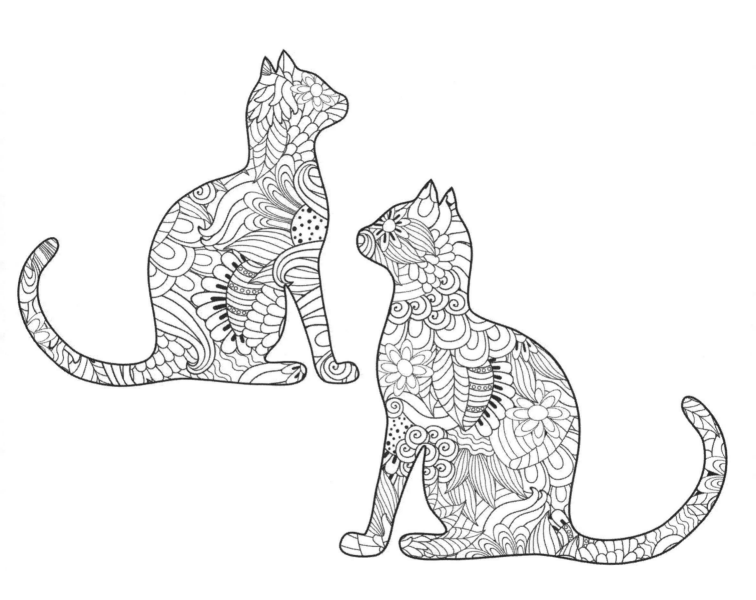

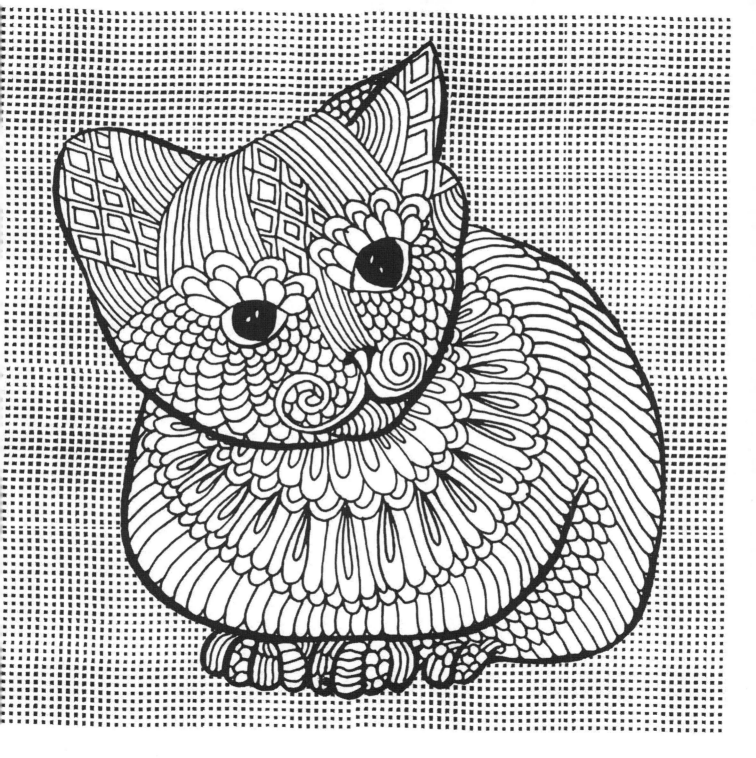

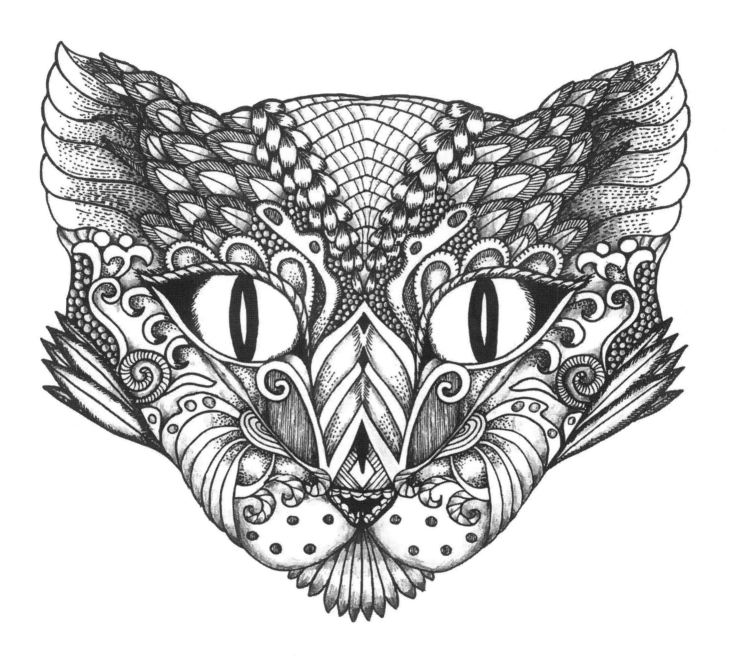

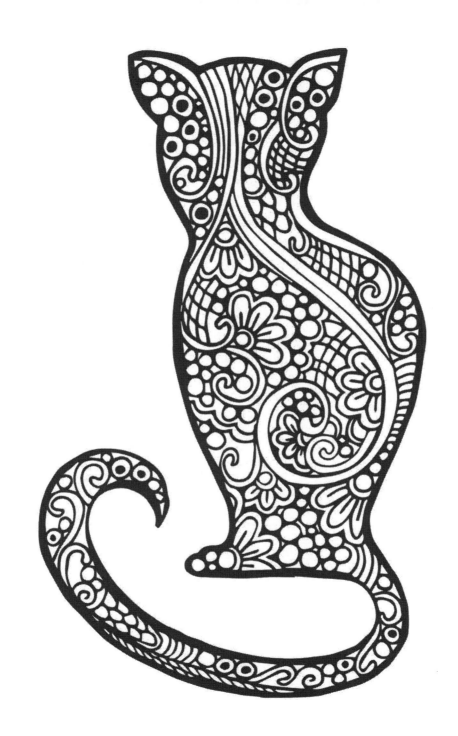

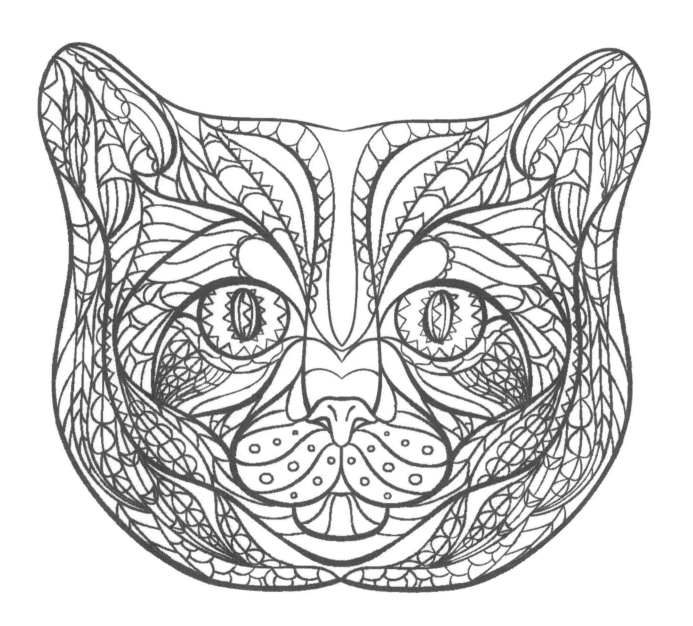

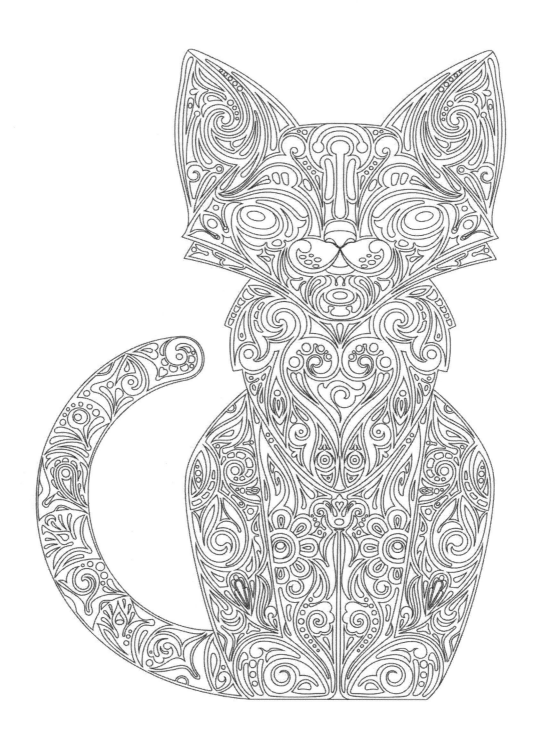

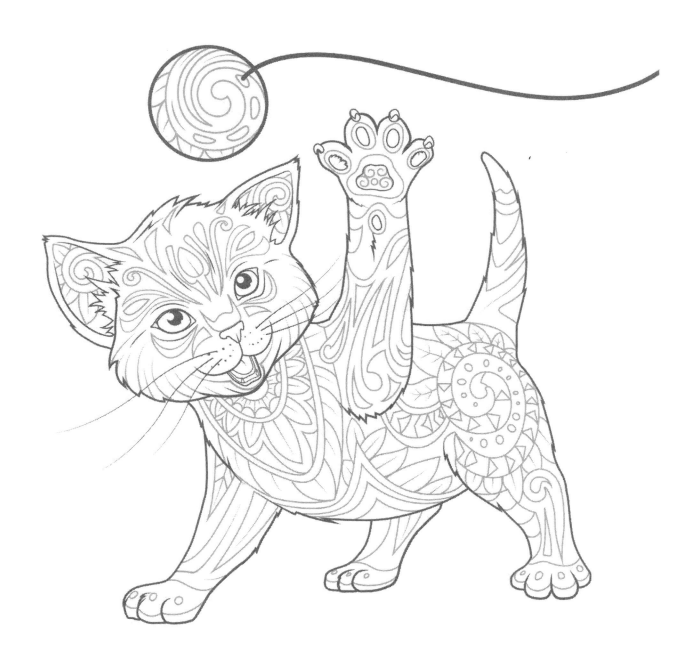

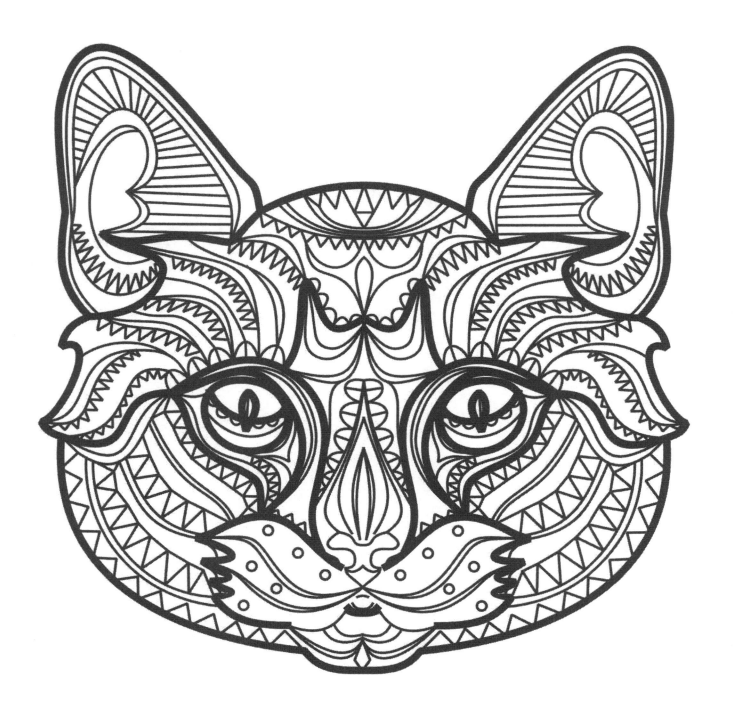

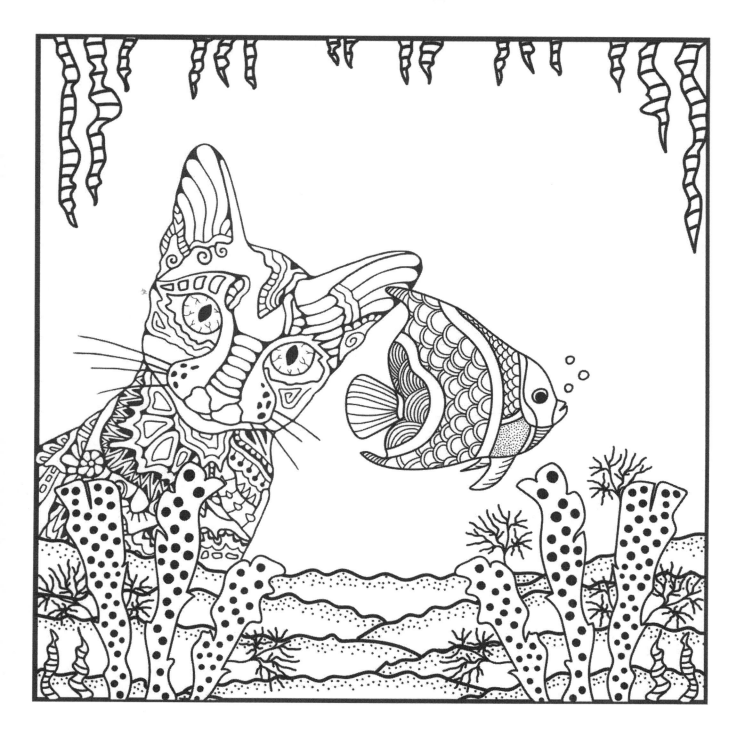

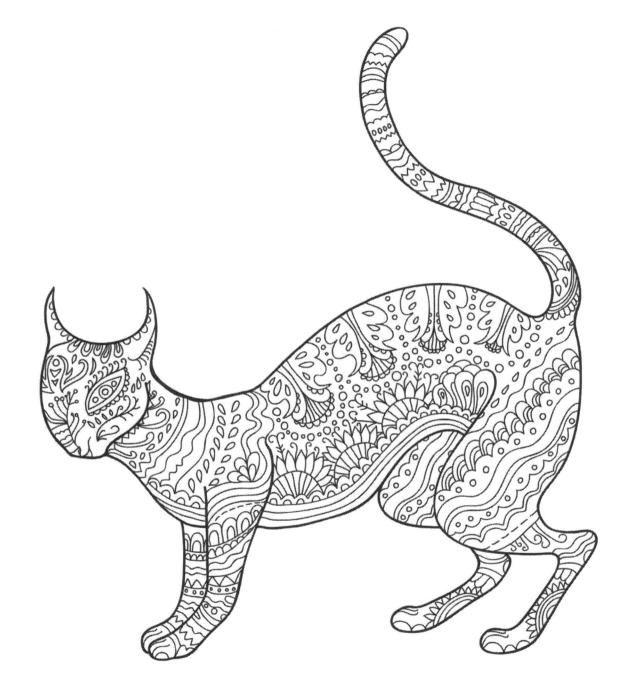

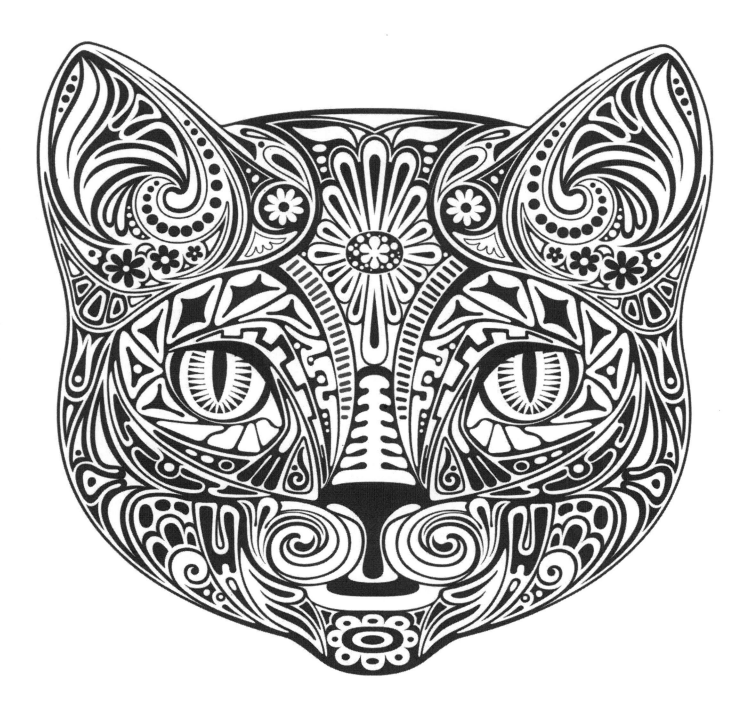

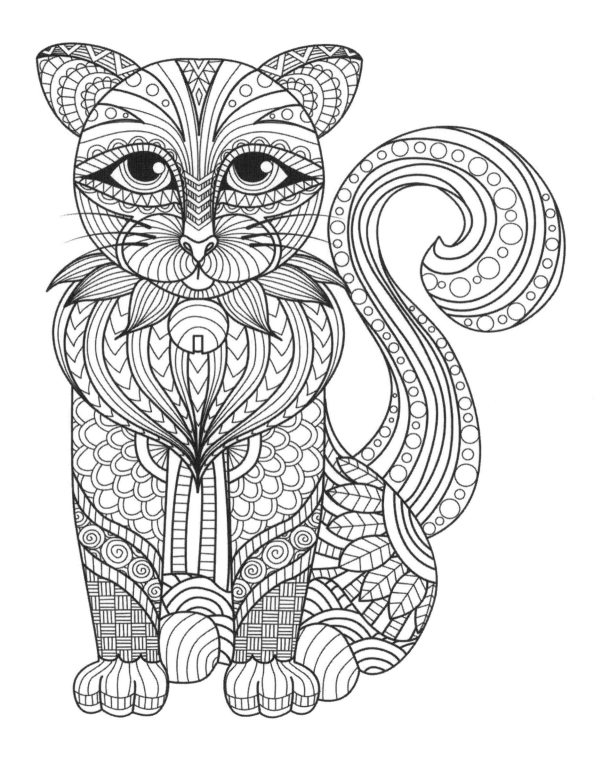

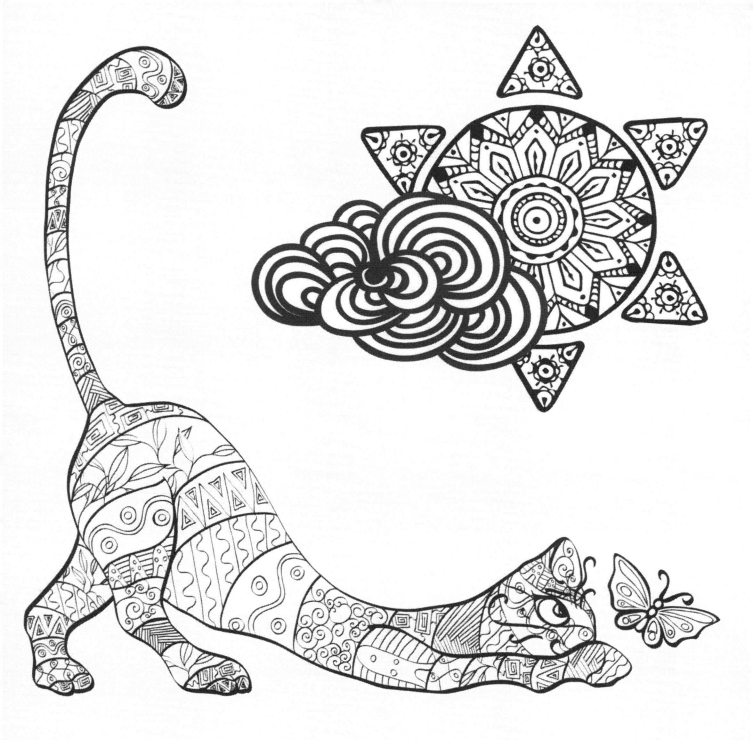

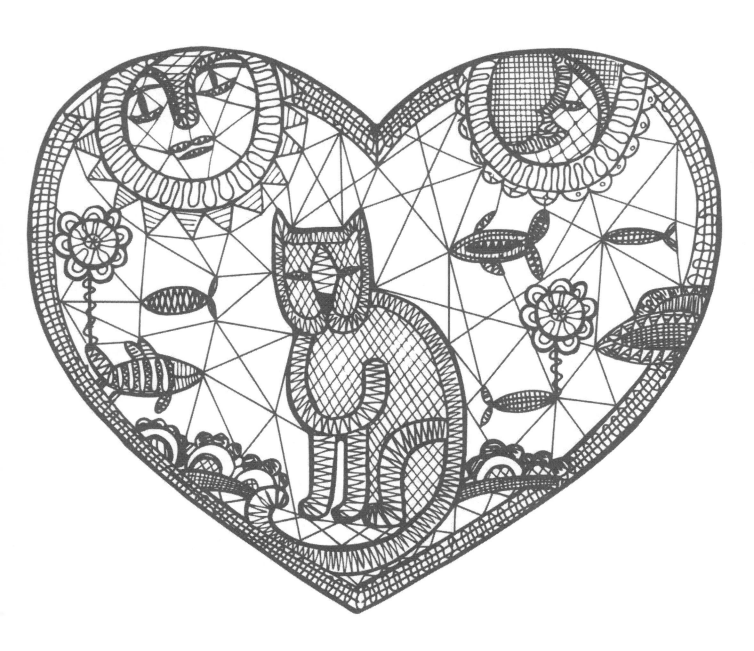

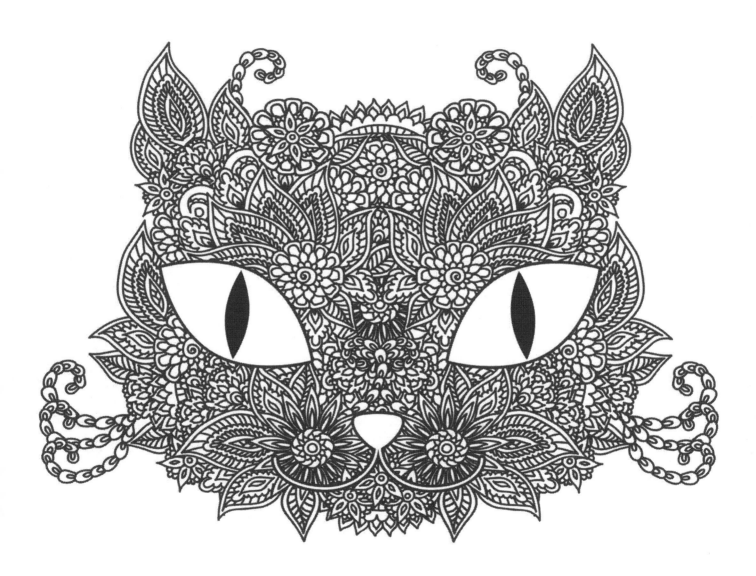

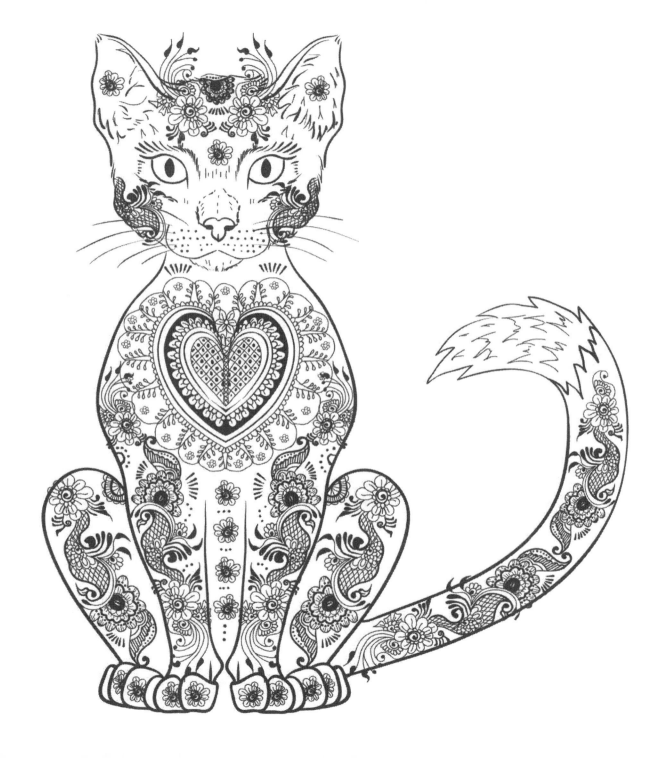

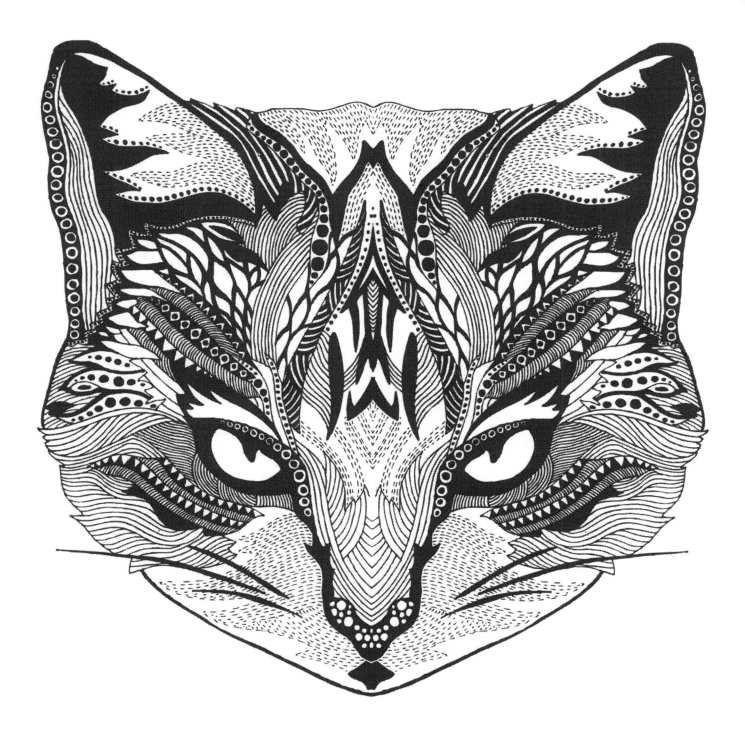

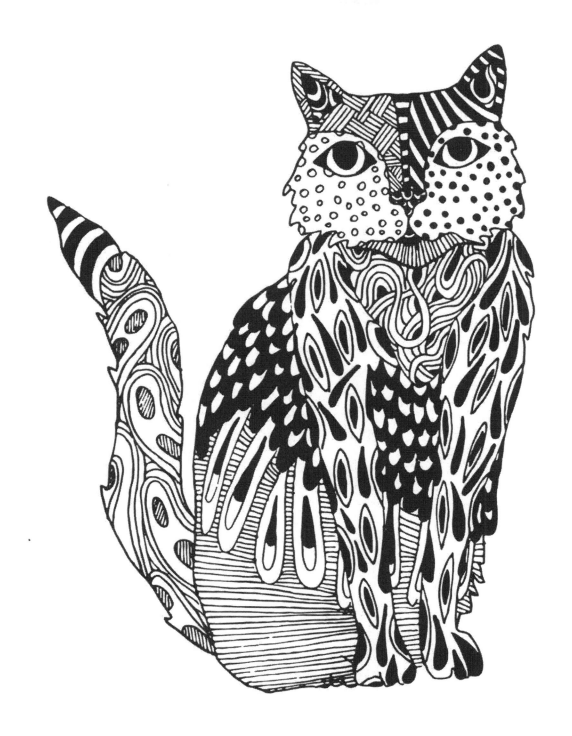

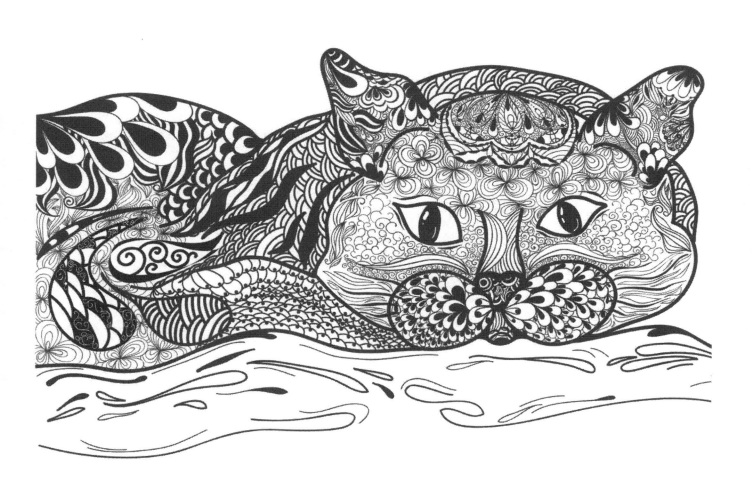

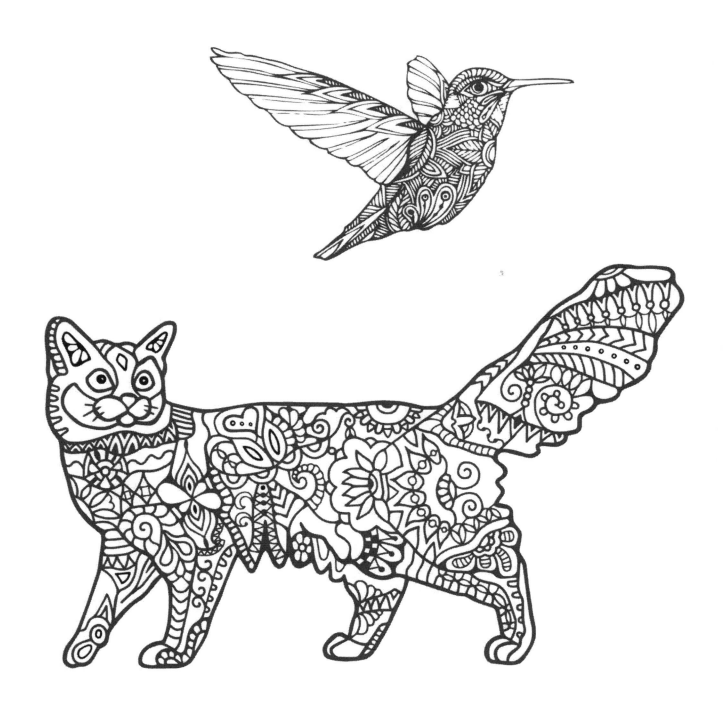

Made in the USA
San Bernardino, CA
12 April 2016